Celebrating Weddings Around the World

Anita Ganeri

heinemann
raintree

Edited by Clare Lewis and Brenda Haugen
Designed by Richard Parker
Picture research by Gina Kammer
Production by Helen McCreath
Originated by Capstone Global Library Ltd
Printed and bound in China by CTPS

19 18 17 16 15
10 9 8 7 6 5 4 3 2 1

Library of Congress Cataloging-in-Publication Data
Ganeri, Anita, 1961-
  Celebrating weddings around the world / Anita Ganeri.
     pages cm.—(Cultures and customs)
  Includes bibliographical references and index.
  ISBN 978-1-4109-8017-5 (hb)—ISBN 978-1-4109-8022-9 (pb)—ISBN 978-1-4109-8032-8 (ebook) 1. Marriage customs and rites—Juvenile literature. 2. Weddings—Juvenile literature. I. Title.
  GT2690.G36 2016
  392.5—dc23   2015000289

Acknowledgments
We would like to thank the following for permission to reproduce photographs:
Alamy: © Danita Delimont, 9, © ephotocorp, 11, © SFM Italy, 13; Capstone Press (map), throughout; Capstone Studio: Karon Dubke, 28, 29; Corbis: Godong/© Robert Mulder, 21; Getty Images: Avinash Achar, 16, Burke/Triolo Productions, 20, Holger Leue, 8, Jodi Cobb, 27, Kevin Winter, 5, Maremagnum, 7; Glow Images: Exotica, 10, PhotoNonStop/Sébastien Boisse, 25, Superstock, 14; Newscom: Jochen Tack imageBROKER, 15, Juan_Herrero European Press Agency, 26, Peter Langer/Design Pics, 17, REUTERS/LEE JAE-WON, 18, REUTERS/MOHAMED AL-SAYAGHI, 19, Robert Harding/Tuul, 6, Robert Harding/Tuul, 12, ZUMAPRESS/Du Boisberranger Jean, 24; Shutterstock: S-F, 23, Sergey Ryzhov, 22, silentwings, cover

We would like to thank Dr. Suzanne Owen for her invaluable help in the preparation of this book.

Every effort has been made to contact copyright holders of material reproduced in this book. Any omissions will be rectified in subsequent printings if notice is given to the publisher.

Contents

Some words are shown in bold, **like this**. You can find out what they mean by looking in the glossary.

Getting Married

In cultures around the world, important events in people's lives are marked with special customs and ceremonies. They help people to celebrate occasions, such as the birth of a baby, a wedding, or remembering a person who has died. They are also a way to guide people from one stage of their lives to the next. This book looks at how people from different cultures and religions celebrate weddings.

All over the world, weddings are happy occasions that the bride and groom often want to share with their friends and family. There are usually special clothes to wear and special foods to eat, including many different types of wedding cakes. In some cultures, people exchange rings or other jewelry. There are also many customs for finding a partner.

OVER THE BROOM

In some African American families, couples end their wedding ceremony by jumping over a broomstick. This tradition dates back to the days of **slavery**, when slaves were not allowed to get married officially. "Jumping the broom" showed that they wanted to be together.

This African American groom and his new wife are "jumping the broom."

Beauty Contest

The Woodabe tribe lives in Niger, West Africa. They are cattle herders who move from place to place to find food and water for their animals. Once a year, they gather together at the edge of the Sahara Desert for a very unusual beauty contest.

Young Woodabe men wear colorful clothes and makeup for their dance.

The young men paint their faces and put on colorful costumes made from beads and shells. Then they stand in lines, link arms, and dance for hours in the hot desert sun. The men roll their eyes to make them look bigger and grin to show off their teeth. They wear black lipstick to make their teeth look whiter. Some men also wear headdresses decorated with ostrich feathers, to make them look taller.

The aim of the contest is to find a woman to marry. The women watch the men dancing and pick who they think is the most handsome as their husbands.

COLOR CODING

The colors of the dancers' makeup have special meanings. Red is the color of blood. Yellow is the color of magic. Black is the opposite of white—the color of death. The black paint is made from the bones of a bird called the **cattle egret**.

Leap of Faith

On the islands of Vanuatu in the South Pacific Ocean, men have a daring way to show off to possible girlfriends. They jump off a wooden tower that is about 98 feet (30 meters) high. They have only two **vines** tied around their ankles to stop them from crashing to the ground. The aim is to swing as low as possible, just grazing their shoulders on the ground. The jumpers hope the more daring they are, the more impressed the women will be.

A jumper leaps from the wooden tower, held up by only two vines.

The tower takes about four weeks to make, with the whole village helping. The ground underneath is dug over to make it softer for landing. Platforms are built at different heights, the lowest at around 33 feet (10 meters) above the ground. On the night before the jump, the men sleep underneath the tower to scare away evil spirits.

GOOD HARVEST

Vine-jumping is also linked to the yearly **yam** harvest, in the months of April, May, and June. Yams are an important food on the island. A good dive is said to bring a good harvest.

On the day of the jump, the men wash and rub themselves with coconut oil. They wear boar tusks around their necks. They cross their arms over their chests and tuck their heads in, to avoid injury. Then they jump, reaching speeds of more than 43 miles (70 kilometers) per hour as they dive.

Villagers gather around the tower, singing and dancing, to show their support for the jumpers.

Sacred Steps

Many **Hindus** marry someone chosen for them by their families, although the boy and girl must agree with their parents' choice. A priest looks at the couple's **horoscopes** and decides on a lucky day for the wedding.

On the wedding day, there are around 15 different **rituals** to be performed. The ceremony is led by a priest who reads from the **sacred** texts and lights the sacred fire. The bride and groom follow the priest's instructions, but they do not speak to each other.

The Hindu bride and groom walk around the sacred fire.

During the ceremony, the priest ties the groom's scarf to the bride's **sari** to show that they are joined for life. The bride places her foot on a special stone to show that she will stand firm for her husband and family.

The most important part of the ceremony comes near the end. The bride and groom take seven steps around the sacred fire. With each step, they make a vow for food, good health, wealth, good fortune, children, happiness, and lifelong friendship. The couple is now married.

WEDDING NECKLACE

To show that she is married, a Hindu bride wears a black and gold necklace. It is called a mangala sutra, which means "lucky thread." She also paints a red mark on her forehead.

This mangala sutra is ready for the wedding ceremony.

Sikh
Wedding

Sikh weddings often take place in the **gurdwara**. The bride and groom bow to the Guru Granth Sahib, the Sikh holy book, before sitting down. The bridegroom wears a long scarf, called a pulla, around his neck. After readings and prayers, the groom takes one end of the pulla and the bride takes the other. This shows that they are now joined together.

During the ceremony, the bride holds one end of the groom's pulla.

During the wedding ceremony, the Lavan (wedding hymn) is read. The four verses are spoken, then sung. As each verse is sung, the bride and groom walk around the Guru Granth Sahib. When they have done this for a fourth time, they are married. The guests shower them with rose petals to congratulate them.

The bride and groom walk around the Guru Granth Sahib.

WEDDING HYMN

This is the first verse of the Lavan:

"In this first circle, God has shown
   you the duties of family life.
Accept the Guru's word as your guide
And it will make you free from sin.
Meditate on the name of God,
Which is the theme of all the scriptures.
Devote yourself to God and all evil
   will go away.
Blessed are those who hold God in
   their hearts.
They are always happy and content."

Shinto
Wedding

Shinto is an ancient religion that many people still follow in Japan. Its followers believe in spirits, called **kami**, that live in animals, plants, and places such as rivers and mountains. They honor the kami at special **shrines**.

Shinto weddings take place at a shrine and are led by a Shinto priest and the miko (female shrine **attendants**). Only close friends and family are invited. At the beginning of the ceremony, everyone stands and bows, and the priest says prayers for the couple.

The bride, groom, priest, miko, and guests make up this Shinto wedding procession.

14

WEARING WHITE

A Shinto bride wears a white **kimono** and a large, white hood. Tradition says that the hood covers up her "horns of jealousy" so that she can start her new life with her husband.

Afterward, the bride and groom drink an alcoholic drink called sake. They take turns sipping from three different-sized cups—small, medium, and large. The first two times, they only raise the cups to their lips. They take a drink on the third time. Then, the couple stands near the **altar**, and the groom reads out the wedding **oath**.

The ceremony ends with the miko giving the couple a **sacred** branch, which they put on the altar as an offering to the kami. They also exchange rings.

This Shinto bride and her groom are wearing traditional dress.

Wedding colors

In Western countries, many brides wear white on their wedding day. In Great Britain, white dresses became very popular after the British queen, Victoria, got married in 1840. The queen wore a white lace dress. Before that, brides had worn many different colors, such as blue, yellow, black, and brown.

In many Eastern cultures, red is a lucky color. A **Hindu** bride usually wears a red silk **sari** because red is the color of blood, and of life itself. Her hands and feet are decorated with delicate patterns, painted in a red dye called mehndi (henna).

A Hindu bride also wears beautiful wedding jewelry.

Wedding rings

Many people exchange gold rings during their weddings, as a sign of their love for each other. They wear the rings on the fourth fingers of their left hands. In ancient times, people thought that a vein led from this finger straight to the heart.

The bride and groom wear crowns during part of the ceremony.

Marriage crowns

In the Eastern Orthodox Church, the bride and groom have beautiful gold crowns placed on their heads. The crowns show that they are now linked to each other and to God. The crowns are taken off at the end of the ceremony.

Mass Wedding

Getting married is one of the most special days in a person's life. Many couples enjoy being the center of attention, with their friends and family helping them to celebrate. Other couples like to get married in large groups, with hundreds of other brides and grooms.

The Unification Church of South Korea holds huge wedding ceremonies for its members.

There are hundreds of brides and grooms at this mass wedding.

CUTTING COSTS

For more than 20 years, mass weddings have been held in Bahrain. In January 2014, 202 couples were married at one time. The weddings are paid for by a charity, to help young couples cut down on their wedding costs.

Grooms line up for a mass wedding in Bahrain.

In February 2000, about 60,000 people got married at a mass wedding held in the Olympic Stadium in Seoul, South Korea. They came from 150 different countries. For thousands of the couples, it was the very first time that the bride and groom had ever met each other.

At the ceremony, the couples were sprinkled with holy water. Then they said their wedding vows and exchanged rings. The ceremony ended with a fireworks display. Until his death in 2012, these mass weddings were led by the church's leader, Reverend Sun Myung Moon. They are now led by his wife, Hak Ja Han.

Breaking Glass

A traditional **Jewish** wedding begins with the bride and groom signing the ketubah (say "kett-oo-bah"), or marriage **contract**. This sets out the promises that the bride and groom make to each other for a long and happy life together.

This Jewish bride and groom are standing under a huppah.

During the ceremony, the couple stands under a special canopy called a huppah. The huppah is a sign of the new home that they will share. It is closed on top for privacy, but open on all sides as a sign that others are welcome inside. The **rabbi** makes a speech about the couple and says seven blessings, one for each of the seven days of creation. He also blesses a glass of wine and gives it to the couple to drink.

The ceremony ends with the groom stomping on a wine glass with his foot. This is said to be a reminder of the destruction of the Temple in Jerusalem, the Jews' holiest place, almost 2,000 years ago. It shows the couple that there will be sad times ahead as well as happiness.

MAZEL TOV!

Afterward, the guests call out "Mazal Tov!," which means "Congratulations!" in **Hebrew**. The day ends with a party, with lots to eat and drink and plenty of singing and dancing.

Everyone joins in the dancing at the wedding party!

Wedding cakes

At weddings in North America and parts of Europe, there is usually a fancy wedding cake. The cake is a sponge or fruit cake, decorated with white icing and often topped with figures of the bride and groom. It is made in different layers. The top layer may be saved for the couple's first anniversary or the christening of their first child.

The bride and groom cut their wedding cake together.

Guests at weddings in Brazil are given "bem casados" ("happily married") cakes to take home. These are made from two pieces of sponge cake, joined together with caramel cream or jam. They show how the couple is joined together as husband and wife.

Chicken soup

In Germany, people eat a special wedding soup called Hochzeitssuppe. It is a clear chicken soup with pieces of chicken, small meatballs, asparagus, noodles, and boiled egg. It is eaten with slices of raisin bread.

Decorated bread

Korovai is a large, round, braided loaf of bread served at weddings in the Ukraine. It is often decorated with birds, which represent the couple and their family and friends. The loaf is surrounded by periwinkle leaves, a symbol of love.

This korovai has periwinkle leaves on it. They are a symbol of love.

Wedding Festival

Every year in September, the Berber people of Morocco hold a special festival in the region of Imilchil, high up in the Atlas Mountains. Thousands of people come from the villages all around to look for husbands and wives. The festival lasts for three days, and people camp out in the valley. There is a **bazaar** where people can buy clothes and other goods, and a market where sheep, goats, and donkeys are sold.

These Berber girls are dressed up for the Imilchil festival.

The grooms sing and dance as they wait to meet their future wives.

At Imilchil, the girls dress up in their finest clothes and best silver jewelry. The boys wear white turbans and long robes. By the end of the festival about 40 couples are ready to get engaged. If a boy and girl like each other, their families meet in a tent to discuss the arrangements for the wedding, which is celebrated another day.

LAKES OF TEARS

There is a sad story behind the festival. Legend says that a boy and girl from different tribes fell in love. However, they were not allowed to marry because their families were enemies. The two cried themselves to death, filling two lakes with their tears. In their grief, their families set up the festival so that boys and girls from different tribes could meet.

Civil Ceremonies

A **civil ceremony** is a wedding that has nothing to do with religion. It can take place in a courthouse or another place that has been registered for weddings, such as a park or hotel. The couple invites their friends and family and may choose readings, poems, music, and songs as part of the ceremony. A civil wedding means that a couple is married according to the law.

Civil ceremonies can even be held in an aquarium!

In some countries, the civil ceremony may be only one part of a wedding. It shows that the couple is legally married, but they may have a religious ceremony, too.

This couple is traveling by helicopter to a wedding in the Grand Canyon.

Some people choose to have their weddings in places that are special to them, such as on a beach or in the countryside. Others choose unusual places to get married, such as in a zoo or aquarium, or deep under the sea, wearing scuba-diving gear.

Fold a Japanese Paper Butterfly

At a Shinto wedding, the bride and groom sip sake from cups decorated with paper butterflies (see page 15). These are some of the oldest origami designs. Follow these steps to make your own paper butterflies.

- rectangle of pretty paper, with a different color or pattern on each side

1 Fold the paper rectangle in half lengthways. Crease and unfold.

2 Fold the paper in half again the other way.

3 Put your thumb inside the top-right corner. Open up the paper and bring the corner across to touch the fold in the middle. Smooth the paper flat, into a triangle shape.

4 Turn the paper over, and do the same on the other side.

5 Turn the shape upside down. Fold the inside corners down, crease, and unfold.

6 Fold down the front layer of paper on each side. Press down to flatten the wings.

Make butterflies in lots of different colors and patterns. Use them to decorate wedding cards and gifts.

Glossary

altar place where offerings such as food and flowers are made to gods and ancestors

attendant person who helps the priest in the Shinto religion

bazaar another word for market

cattle egret small bird that picks ticks and flies from cattle

civil ceremony ceremony that is not religious, but is legally binding

contract agreement between people

gurdwara Sikh place of worship

Hebrew language in which the Jewish holy books are written

Hindu person who follows the Hindu religion

horoscope chart showing the position of the stars and planets at the time of a baby's birth

Jewish connected with the religion of Judaism. A Jew is a person who follows Judaism.

kami spirits in the Shinto religion that are found in nature

kimono traditional Japanese silk dress

oath solemn promise

rabbi Jewish religious teacher

ritual ceremony with set ways of doing things

sacred special, usually relating to religion

sari traditional dress worn by many women in India

shrine holy place linked to a religious leader, god, or saint

Sikh person who follows the Sikh religion

slavery when people are forced to work for others for no money and are owned by them. In the past, people from Africa were taken to the United States and forced to work as slaves.

vines plants with long, dangling stems

yam plant that has underground parts called tubers that can be eaten

Find Out More

Books

Jones, Aled. *What Do You Believe?: Religion and Faith in the World Today.* New York: Dorling Kindersley, 2011.

Meredith, Susan. *The Usbourne Encyclopedia of World Religions* (Internet-Linked Encyclopedias). Tulsa, OK.: EDC, 2010.

Rohr, Ian. *Religious Celebrations* (Celebrations). Mankato, MN.: Smart Apple Media, 2011.

Web sites

Facthound offers a safe, fun way to find Internet sites related to this book. All of the sites on Facthound have been researched by our staff.

Here's all you do:

Visit www.facthound.com

Type in this code: 9781410980175

Further research

Have you ever been to a wedding? What was the ceremony like? Can you find out more about how people celebrate weddings around the world? What do the bride and groom wear? What do people eat? You can look in books, on the Internet, or ask your friends.

Index